D' Artagnan Grimm's Erotic Fairy Tales

BEN
DUNN
2011

BEN DUNN 2012

Gotham Gazzette
BATMAN CATCHES CLUEMASTER
SAVAGE ROOFTOP BATTLE
JOK

©Kenny Kiernan

12
3

FOUST©

Foust©

FOUST

09'17
© 2017 SHAMINE A. KING
QUARTERVIRUS

ME

www.ingramcontent.com/pod-product-compliance
Lightning Source LLC
Chambersburg PA
CBHW050326220526
45465CB00005B/2155
* 9 7 9 8 5 9 4 3 5 1 9 2 9 *